LOVE GOD
AND
LOVE ONE ANOTHER

100 Ways to Live Gods Greatest Commandments

STEVEN ANDREW
PASTOR OF USA CHRISTIAN CHURCH

www.USA.church

ACTS ONE EIGHT Publishing

LOVE GOD
AND
LOVE ONE ANOTHER
100 Ways to Live Gods Greatest Commandments

STEVEN ANDREW
PASTOR OF USA CHRISTIAN CHURCH

www.USA.church

ISBN 9780977955039

Copyright © 2011 by Steven Andrew

Published by ACTS ONE EIGHT Publishing
ActsOneEightPublishing.com

Scripture quotations are from the King James Version of the Holy Bible and are marked "KJV". References to God are capitalized. The first letter of a verse is also capitalized. Brackets in verses or quotations are by the author for use as clarification. Other Scriptures are from the TrueKJV™ Holy Bible.

References given in this book do not constitute an endorsement. This book provides information to readers. It is sold and/or provided with the understanding that the publisher and author are not engaged to render any type of legal advice. Your actions are your responsibility. The book may be updated from time to time. Web sites and information listed in this book may change.

Contents

Preface

Reading "Love God and Love One Another" will help bring God's blessings to you. The reason is when you do God's greatest commandments, He favors you. This book is based on the Holy Bible, so you have confidence in what God says.

The Bible is the number one best selling book of all time; it alone is God's Word. No other book is like it. God's Word is eternal. When you read God's Word, He speaks to you.

If you haven't started yet, will you begin praying to God and reading the Bible each morning and evening? If you ask God for the Holy Spirit to help you understand His Word, God will answer your prayer (Mark 11:24).

Always remember, Jesus loves you.

Steven Andrew
Pastor of USA Christian Church
One Nation Under God
"Blessed is the nation whose God is the LORD" Psalm 33:12

Web site: www.USA.church

෴

I thank God for each person who reviewed the manuscript. Your suggestions have made this a better book. I appreciate you; God delights in you. May God strengthen you in Jesus' name!

1

100 Ways to Love God

Father,
I love You with all my heart, and with all my soul,
and with all my mind, and with all my strength.
In Jesus' name. Amen.

Jesus Christ gave us the first of God's two Greatest Commandments in Mark 12:30. He said:

"You shall love the Lord your God with all your heart, and with all your soul, and with all your mind, and with all your strength."

According to our Lord, your first priority is to love God. He loves you and He created you to love Him.

Do you know that something miraculous happens when you love God? What is extraordinary is that as you draw near to God, He draws near to you (James 4:8). You can pray, *Father, I draw near to You through Jesus Christ Your Son.* By praying this simple prayer, God draws near to you. As an inspirational and practical tool, here are one hundred ways from the Word of God how to love God.

100 Ways to Love God

❧ <u>Obey the First Commandment</u> ❧

1. **"You shall love the Lord your God with all your heart"** (innermost being) *Mark 12:30 KJV*

2. **"... with all your soul"** (emotions, will...) *Mark 12:30 KJV*

3. **"... with all your mind"** (thoughts, intellect...) *Mark 12:30 KJV*

4. **"... with all your strength"** (what you do, how you live...)" *Mark 12:30 KJV*

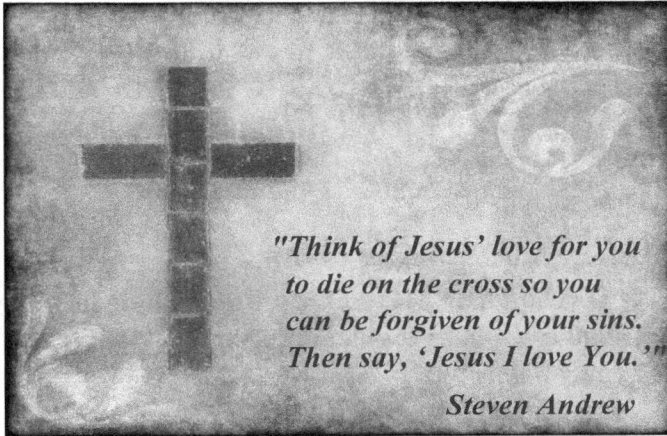

> *"Think of Jesus' love for you to die on the cross so you can be forgiven of your sins. Then say, 'Jesus I love You.'"*
>
> *Steven Andrew*

❧ Daily Living ❧

5. *Draw near to God*

   "Draw near to God, and He will draw near to you." *James 4:8*

6. *Seek the things which are of Christ Jesus*

   "For all seek their own, not the things which are Jesus Christ's." *Philippians 2:21 KJV*

7. *Keep God's commandments*

   "He that has My commandments, and keeps them, he it is that loves Me." *John 14:21*

8. *To love God is to obey the Holy Bible*

   "If ye love Me, keep My commandments." *John 14:15 KJV*

9. *Make disciples of Jesus Christ*

   "Teaching them to observe all things whatever I have commanded you" *Matthew 28:19*

10. *Abide (dwell) in Jesus Christ*

"If ye abide in Me, and My words abide in you, ye shall ask what ye will, and it shall be done unto you." *John 15:7 KJV*

11. *Think of God's grace*

"For by grace are ye saved through faith; and that not of yourselves: it is the gift of God: Not of works, lest any man should boast." *Eph. 2:8-9 KJV*

12. *Hate evil*

"The fear of the LORD is to hate evil" *Proverbs 8:13 KJV*

13. *Share that Jesus Christ rose from the dead*

"Christ died for our sins according to the scriptures; And that He was buried, and that He rose again the third day according to the scriptures" *1 Corinthians 15:3-4 KJV*

14. *Contend earnestly for the faith*

"Earnestly contend for the faith which was once delivered unto the saints." *Jude 3 KJV*

15. *Read the whole Bible*

"Your word is true from the beginning: and every one of Your righteous judgments endures for ever." *Psalm 119:160*

16. *Nourish the body of Christ (the church)*
"Feed My sheep." *John 21:17 KJV*

17. *Do everything as to the Lord*

"Whatsoever ye do, do it heartily, as to the Lord, and not unto men" *Colossians 3:23 KJV*

18. *Break all ties with the occult*

"Regard not them that have familiar spirits, neither seek after wizards, to be defiled by them: I am the LORD your God." *Leviticus 19:31 KJV* **"The soul that turns after such as have familiar spirits, and after wizards, to go a whoring after them, I will even set My face against that soul, and will cut him off from among his people."** *Leviticus 20:6*

19. *Be pure in heart*

"Blessed are the pure in heart: for they shall see God." *Matthew 5:8 KJV*

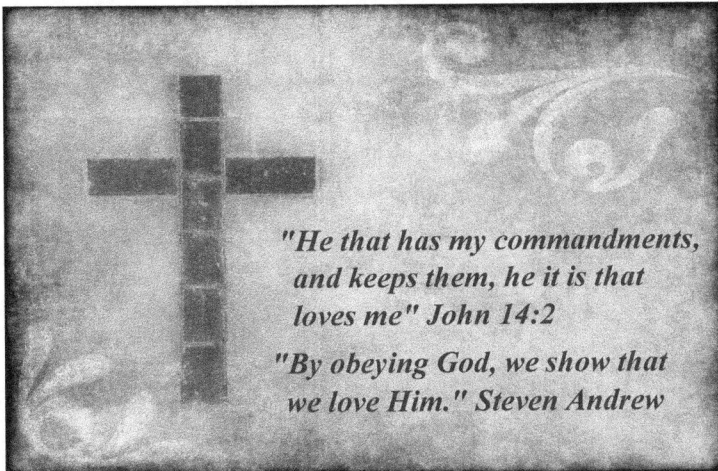

"He that has my commandments, and keeps them, he it is that loves me" John 14:2

"By obeying God, we show that we love Him." Steven Andrew

9

20. *Live by faith in Jesus Christ*

"I am crucified with Christ: nevertheless I live; yet not I, but Christ lives in me: and the life which I now live in the flesh I live by the faith of the Son of God, who loved me, and gave Himself for me." *Galatians 2:20*

21. *Be glad in God*

"Serve the LORD with gladness" *Psalm 100:2*

22. *Pray an hour or more with Jesus*

"Watch and pray, that ye enter not into temptation: the spirit indeed is willing, but the flesh is weak." *Matthew 26:40 KJV*

23. *Believe God*

"Abraham believed God, and it was accounted unto him for righteousness." *Romans 4:3 KJV*

24. *Get equipped for every good work with the Holy Bible*

"All scripture is given by inspiration of God, and is profitable for doctrine, for reproof, for correction, for instruction in righteousness: That the man of God may be perfect, thoroughly furnished unto all good works. *2 Timothy 3:16-17*

25. *Be filled with the Spirit*

"Be filled with the Spirit; Speaking to yourselves in psalms and hymns and spiritual songs, singing and making melody in your heart to the Lord; Giving thanks always for all things unto God and the Father in the name of our Lord Jesus Christ; *Ephesians 5:18-20 KJV*

26. *Keep the unity of the Spirit*

"Endeavoring to keep the unity of the Spirit in the bond of peace." *Ephesians 4:3*

❧ Names of God ☙

God has revealed Himself by sharing His names. A partial list follows. Prayerfully and personally know God as:

27. *Elohim, "Creator"*

"In the beginning God [Elohim] created the heaven and the earth." *Genesis 1:1 KJV*

28. *Jehovah, "my Lord God"... Covenant*

"And the LORD [Jehovah] God formed man of the dust of the ground, and breathed into his nostrils the breath of life; and man became a living soul." *Genesis 2:7 KJV*

29. *Adonai, "Master and Lord"*

"Abram said, Lord [Adonai] GOD, what will you give me, seeing I go childless, and the steward of my house is this Eliezer of Damascus?" *Genesis 15:2 KJV*

30. *El Shaddai, "God Almighty, my Supply, my Nourishment"*

"When Abram was ninety years old and nine, the LORD appeared to Abram, and said unto him, I am the Almighty God [El Shaddai]; walk before Me, and be you perfect. And I will make My covenant between Me and you, and will multiply you exceedingly." *Genesis 17:1-2*

31. *Jehovah Jireh, "the Lord my Provider"*

   "Abraham called the name of that place Jehovahjireh: as it is said to this day, In the mount of the LORD it shall be seen." *Genesis 22:14 KJV*

32. *Jehovah Rapha, "the Lord who heals"*

   "For I am the LORD [Jehovah Rapha] **that heals you."** *Exodus 15:26*

33. *Jehovah Nissi, "the Lord my Victory"*

   "Moses built an altar, and called the name of it Jehovahnissi" *Exodus 17:15 KJV*

34. *Jehovah Mikadesh, "Sanctifier"*

   "Sanctify yourselves therefore, and be ye holy: for I am the LORD your God. And ye shall keep My statutes, and do them: I am the LORD which sanctify [Mikadesh] **you."** *Leviticus 20:7-8 KJV*

35. *Jehovah Tsidkenu, "the Lord who is our Righteousness"*

   "This is His name whereby He shall be called, THE LORD OUR RIGHTEOUSNESS [Jehovah Tsidkenu]**."** *Jeremiah 23:6 KJV*

36. *Jehovah Shalom, "the Lord my peace"*

   "Then Gideon built an altar there unto the LORD, and called it Jehovahshalom" *Judges 6:24 KJV*

37. *Jehovah Rohi, "my Shepherd"*

   "The LORD [Jehovah Rohi] **is my shepherd; I shall not want."** *Psalm 23:1 KJV*

38. *Jehovah Shammah, "the Lord is there"*

   "The name of the city from that day shall be, THE LORD IS THERE [Jehovah Shammah]**."** *Ezekiel 48:35 KJV*

39. *Father*

    "Our Father" *Luke 11:2 KJV*

40. *Jesus as your Lord and Savior*

    "Grow in grace, and in the knowledge of our Lord and Saviour Jesus Christ." *2 Peter 3:18 KJV*

41. *Jesus as your friend*

    "I have called you friends; for all things that I have heard of my Father I have made known unto you." *John 15:15 KJV*

42. *The Holy Spirit as your Comforter*

    "But the Comforter, which is the Holy Ghost, whom the Father will send in My name, He shall teach you all things, and bring all things to your remembrance, whatever I have said unto you." *John 14:26*

13

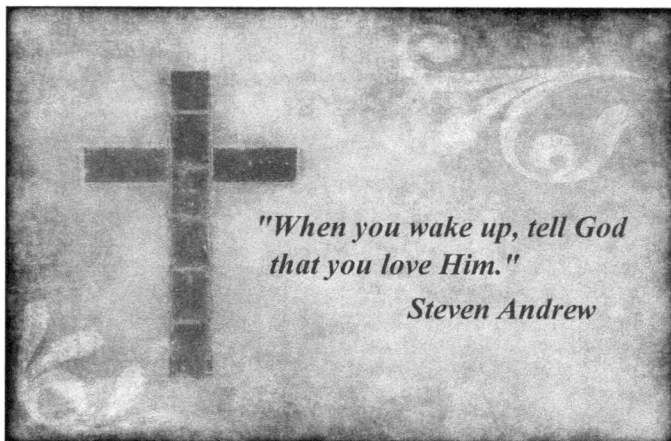

"When you wake up, tell God that you love Him."

Steven Andrew

❧ Thanksgiving. Praise… ☙

43. *Thank God*

   "Enter into His gates with thanksgiving"
   Psalm 100:4 KJV

44. *Praise the Lord*

   "Praise the Lord; for His mercy endures forever."
   2 Chronicles 20:21

45. *Bless the Lord*

   "Bless the LORD, O my soul, and forget not all His benefits" *Psalm 103:2 KJV*

46. *Shout to the Lord*

   "Make a joyful shout to the LORD, all you lands!"
   Psalm 100:1

47. *Sing to God*

   "Sing unto Him a new song" *Psalm 33:3 KJV*

48. *Rejoice in the Lord*

   "Rejoice in the Lord always" *Philippians 4:4*

49. *Make the Lord your dwelling place*

   **"Because you have made the LORD, which is my
   refuge, even the most High, your habitation; There
   shall no evil befall you, neither shall any plague
   come near your dwelling."** *Psalm 91:9-10*

50. *Hear from God every day*

   **"It is written, Man shall not live by bread alone,
   but by every word that proceeds out of the mouth
   of God."** *Matthew 4:4*

51. *Thank Jesus Christ for saving you*

   **"There shall in no wise enter into it any thing that
   defile, neither whatever works abomination, or
   makes a lie: but they which are written in the
   Lamb's book of life."** *Revelation 21:27*

52. *Say, "I love the Lord"*

   **"I love the LORD, because He has heard my voice
   and my supplications."** *Psalm 116:1*

53. *Delight yourself in the Lord*

   **"Delight yourself also in the LORD; and He shall
   give you the desires of your heart."** *Psalm 37:4*

54. *First Commandment*

"You shall have no other gods before Me."
Exodus 20:3

55. *Second Commandment*

"You shall not make unto you any graven image,
or any likeness of any thing that is in heaven
above, or that is in the earth beneath, or that is in
the water under the earth: You shall not bow down
yourself to them, nor serve them: for I the LORD
your God am a jealous God, visiting the iniquity of
the fathers upon the children unto the third and
fourth generation of them that hate Me; And
showing mercy unto thousands of them that love
Me, and keep My commandments." *Exodus 20:4-6*

56. *Third Commandment*

"You shall not take the name of the LORD your
God in vain; for the LORD will not hold him
guiltless that takes His name in vain." *Exodus 20:7*

57. *Fourth Commandment*

"Remember the sabbath day, to keep it holy. Six
days shall you labor, and do all your work: But the
seventh day is the sabbath of the LORD your God:
in it you shall not do any work, you, nor your son,
nor your daughter, your manservant, nor your
maidservant, nor your cattle, nor your stranger
that is within your gates: For in six days the LORD
made heaven and earth, the sea, and all that in
them is, and rested the seventh day: For which
reason the LORD blessed the sabbath day, and
hallowed it. *Exodus 20:8-11*

58. *Fifth Commandment*

    "Honor your father and your mother: that your days may be long upon the land which the LORD your God is giving you." *Exodus 20:12*

59. *Sixth Commandment*

    "You shall not kill." *Exodus 20:13*

60. *Seventh Commandment*

    "You shall not commit adultery." *Exodus 20:14*

61. *Eighth Commandment*

    "You shall not steal." *Exodus 20:15*

62. *Ninth Commandment*

    "You shall not bear false witness against your neighbor." *Exodus 20:16*

63. *Tenth Commandment*

    "You shall not covet your neighbor's house, you shall not covet your neighbor's wife, nor his manservant, nor his maidservant, nor his ox, nor his donkey, nor anything that is your neighbor's." *Exodus 20:17*

George Washington Praying at Valley Forge

> *"We do hereby dedicate this Land, (America) and ourselves, to reach the People within these shores with the Gospel of Jesus Christ... May this Covenant of Dedication remain to all generations.... May all who see this Cross, remember what we have done here..."*
> **Jamestown Settlers, Covenant, 1607**

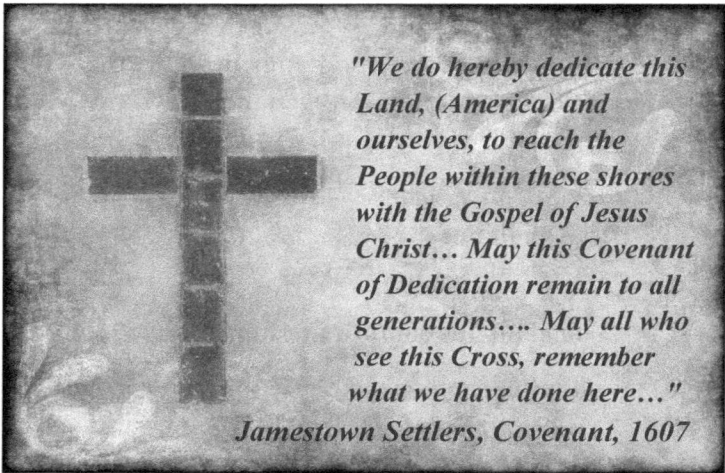

❧ Make a Strong Christian Nation ❧

64. *Affirm: The Lord is God of the USA and we are His people*

    "I will be their God, and they shall be My people." *2 Corinthians 6:16 KJV*

    "Blessed is the nation whose God is the Lord; and the people whom He has chosen for His own inheritance." *Psalm 33:12 KJV*

65. *Affirm Jesus is King of the USA (An American Revolution motto is: "No King But King Jesus")*

    "For God is the King of all the earth" *Psalm 47:7 KJV*

66. *Affirm the Lord is the USA's government (Our Founding Fathers established the USA with Isaiah 33:22)*

    "For the LORD is our judge [Judicial]**, the LORD is our lawgiver** [Legislative]**, the LORD is our king** [Executive]**; He will save us."** *Isaiah 33:22 KJV*

18

67. *Build the USA on the Holy Bible*

"Therefore whoever hears these sayings of Mine, and does them, I will liken him unto a wise man, which built his house upon a rock: And the rain descended, the floods came, and the winds blew and beat on that house; and it fell not: for it was founded upon a rock." *Matthew 7:24-25*

68. *Pursue righteousness in the USA*

"Righteousness exalts a nation: but sin is a reproach to any people." *Proverbs 14:34*

69. *Elect God Fearing Governments*

"He that rules over men must be just, ruling in the fear of God." *2 Samuel 23:3*

"Moreover you shall provide out of all the people able men, such as fear God, men of truth, hating covetousness; and place such over them, to be rulers of thousands, and rulers of hundreds, rulers of fifties, and rulers of tens" *Exodus 18:21*

Congress Seeking God: George Washington (center in black), John Adams (sixth from top left), Samuel Adams (light coat), Benjamin Franklin (second from to right) and Patrick Henry (first on left kneeling)

70. *Sigh and cry over the abominations that are done within the USA*

"The LORD said unto him, Go through the midst of the city, through the midst of Jerusalem, and set a mark upon the foreheads of the men that sigh and that cry for all the abominations that be done in the midst thereof." *Ezekiel 9:4 KJV*

71. *Repent of Personal and National Sin*

"If My people, which are called by My name, shall humble themselves, and pray, and seek My face, and turn from their wicked ways; then will I hear from heaven, and will forgive their sin, and will heal their land." *2 Chronicles 7:14 KJV*

❧ Holiness ❧

72. *Take up your cross and follow Jesus Christ*

"He that takes not his cross, and follows after Me, is not worthy of Me." *Matthew 10:38 KJV*

73. *Seek God's way of escape out of temptation*

"There hath no temptation taken you but such as is common to man: but God is faithful, who will not suffer you to be tempted above that ye are able; but will with the temptation also make a way to escape, that ye may be able to bear it." *1 Corinthians 10:13 KJV*

74. *Be led by the Spirit of God*

    "For as many as are led by the Spirit of God, they are the sons of God." *Romans 8:14 KJV*

75. *Seek first the Kingdom of God and His righteousness*

    "Seek ye first the kingdom of God, and His righteousness; and all these things shall be added unto you." *Matthew 6:33 KJV*

76. *Come to God with boldness because of Jesus' blood*

    "Having therefore, brethren, boldness to enter into the holiest by the blood of Jesus," *Hebrews 10:19 KJV*

77. *Be bold about your faith in Jesus Christ*

    "For I am not ashamed of the gospel of Christ: for it is the power of God unto salvation to every one that believes; to the Jew first, and also to the Greek." *Romans 1:16*

78. *Do not love the world or the things in the world*

    "Love not the world, neither the things that are in the world." *1 John 2:15 KJV*

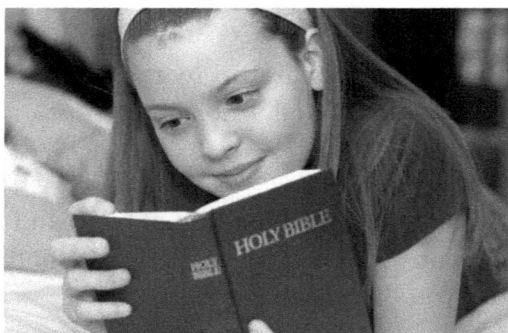

79. *Lay aside every weight and sin*

"Let us lay aside every weight, and the sin which does so easily beset us, and let us run with patience the race that is set before us" *Hebrews 12:1*

80. *Look unto Jesus*

"Looking unto Jesus the author and finisher of our faith" *Hebrews 12:2 KJV*

81. *Show your faith by obeying God*

"Even so faith, if it has not works, is dead, being alone." *James 2:17*

82. *Put to death your sinful nature*

"Put off concerning the former conduct the old man, which is corrupt according to the deceitful lusts" *Ephesians 4:22*

83. *Live holy*

"Neither do I condemn you: go, and sin no more." *John 8:11 KJV*

84. *Seek those things above*

"Seek those things which are above, where Christ sits on the right hand of God." *Colossians 3:1*

85. *Fear God*

"The fear of the LORD is the beginning of knowledge: but fools despise wisdom and instruction." *Proverbs 1:7 KJV*

86. *Press toward the call of God in Christ Jesus*

"I press toward the mark for the prize of the high calling of God in Christ Jesus." *Phil. 3:14 KJV*

87. *Confess: "Jesus Christ is Lord"*

"That every tongue should confess that Jesus Christ is Lord, to the glory of God the Father." *Philippians 2:9 KJV*

88. *Humble yourself under the mighty hand of God*

"Humble yourselves therefore under the mighty hand of God, that He may exalt you in due time: Casting all your care upon Him; for He cares for you." *1 Peter 5:6-7*

President Lincoln taking oath on the Holy Bible

23

89. *Confess your sins to God*

"If we confess our sins, He is faithful and just to forgive us our sins, and to cleanse us from all unrighteousness." *1 John 1:9 KJV*

90. *Separate from those who refuse to obey God*

"Put away from among yourselves the wicked person" *1 Corinthians 5:13 KJV*

91. *Hide God's Word in your heart*

"With what shall a young man cleanse his way? by taking heed according to Your word... Your word I have hid in my heart, that I might not sin against You." *Psalm 119:9, 11*

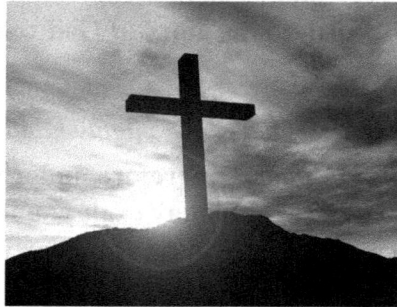

❧ Faith and Miracles ❧

92. *Trust in the Lord with all your heart*

"Trust in the LORD with all your heart; and lean not unto your own understanding." *Proverbs 3:5 KJV*

93. *In all your ways acknowledge God*

"In all your ways acknowledge Him, and He shall direct your paths." *Proverbs 3:6 KJV*

94. *Speak to your mountains to be cast into the sea*

"For verily I say unto you, That whoever shall say unto this mountain, Be you removed, and be you cast into the sea; and shall not doubt in his heart, but shall believe that those things which he says shall come to pass; he shall have whatever he says." *Mark 11:23*

95. *Believe that you receive what you ask in prayer*

"What things soever ye desire, when ye pray, believe that ye receive them, and ye shall have them." *Mark 11:24 KJV*

"Believe God will help you. Miracles are easy for God."
Steven Andrew

96. *Believe God will reward you*

"But without faith it is impossible to please Him: for he that comes to God must believe that He is, and that He is a rewarder of them that diligently seek Him." *Hebrews 11:6*

97. *Rely on God to help you*

   "Were not the Ethiopians and the Lubims a huge army, with very many chariots and horsemen? yet, because you did rely on the LORD, He delivered them into your hand." *2 Chronicles 16:8*

98. *Continually say, meditate and observe God's Word*

   "This book of the law shall not depart out of your mouth; but you shall meditate therein day and night, that you may observe to do according to all that is written therein: for then you shall make your way prosperous, and then you shall have good success." *Joshua 1:8*

99. *Know with God all things are possible*

   "With God all things are possible." *Mark 10:27 KJV*

100. *Know the Lord is God*

   "Be still, and know that I am God" *Psalm 46:10 KJV*

2

100 Ways to Love One Another

Father,

I want to love others as Jesus loved me.

In Jesus' name. Amen.

B y this we know love: Jesus laid down His life for us (1 John 3:16). As Christians we are to do the same. In Mark 12:31, Jesus gives us the second of God's Greatest Commandments. He says,

"You shall love your neighbor as yourself."

Look at Jesus Christ. Do you see His perfect love? Jesus strengthens families. He encourages the weak and weary. His compassion heals the sick. He is faithful. He will never leave you, nor forsake you. Jesus Christ is the Good Samaritan who helps you.

Let's walk in love as Jesus showed us. Here are one hundred ways how to love one another from God's Word.

100 Ways to Love One Another

1. *Love your neighbor as yourself*

   "You shall love your neighbor as yourself."
   Mark 12:31

2. *As Jesus loved you, love one another*

   "Love one another; as I have loved you"
   John 13:34 KJV

୬ Forgiveness and Mercy ୬

3. *Forgive*

   "Forbearing one another, and forgiving one another, if any man have a quarrel against any: even as Christ forgave you, so also do ye."
   Colossians 3:13 KJV

4. *Be merciful*

   "Blessed are the merciful: for they shall obtain mercy." *Matthew 5:7 KJV*

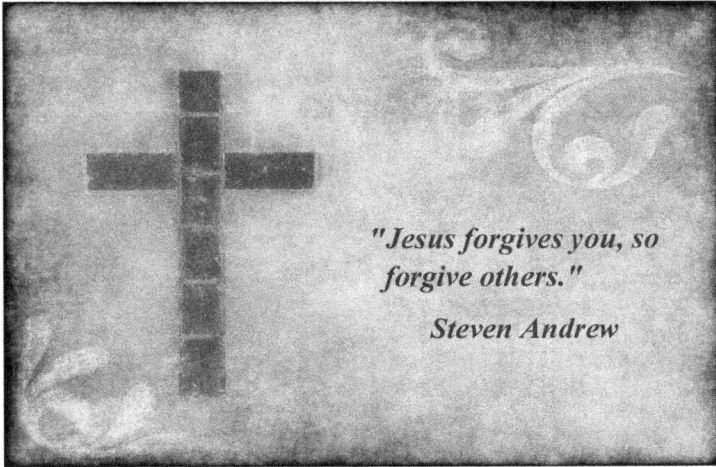

"Jesus forgives you, so forgive others."

Steven Andrew

❧ 1 Corinthians 13 ❧

5. *Be kind*

   "Love suffers long, and is kind" *1 Corinthians 13:4*

6. *Do not envy*

   "Love envies not" *1 Corinthians 13:4*

7. *Do not boast*

   "Love boasts not of itself" *1 Corinthians 13:4*

8. *Do not be puffed up*

   "[Love] is not puffed up" *1 Corinthians 13:4*

9. *Do not behave unbecomingly*

   "[Love] does not behave itself unseemly"
   1 Corinthians 13:5

10. *Do not seek your own*

    "[Love] seeks not her own" *1 Cor.13:5*

29

11. *Do not be provoked*

    "[Love] is not easily provoked"
    1 Corinthians 13:5

12. *Think no evil*

    "[Love] thinks no evil" *1 Corinthians 13:5*

13. *Do not rejoice in iniquity*

    "[Love] rejoices not in iniquity" *1 Cor. 13:6*

14. *Rejoice in the truth*

    "[Love] rejoices in the truth" *1 Corinthians 13:6*

15. *Bear all things*

    "[Love] bears all things" *1 Corinthians 13:7*

16. *Believe all things*

    "[Love] believes all things" *1 Corinthians 13:7*

17. *Hope all things*

    "[Love] hopes all things" *1 Corinthians 13:7*

18. *Endure all things*

    "[Love] endures all things." *1 Corinthians 13:7*

19. *Never fail*

    "Love never fails." *1 Corinthians 13:8*

❧ Relationships ❧

20. *Look out for the interests of others*

   "Look not every man on his own things, but every man also on the things of others."
   Philippians 2:4 KJV

21. *Follow after love*

   "Follow after love" *1 Corinthians 14:1 KJV*

22. *Preach repentance*

   "That repentance and remission of sins should be preached in His name" *Luke 24:47 KJV*

23. *Bear one another's burdens*

   "If it be possible, as much as lies in you, live peaceably with all men." *Romans 12:18 KJV*

24. *Comfort and edify one another*

   "Comfort yourselves together, and edify one another" *1 Thessalonians 5:11 KJV*

"Remember Jesus Christ lives in every Christian."

Steven Andrew

25. *Comfort one another about Jesus Christ's return*

"We which are alive and remain unto the coming of the Lord shall not precede them which are asleep. For the Lord Himself shall descend from heaven with a shout, with the voice of the archangel, and with the trump of God: and the dead in Christ shall rise first: Then we which are alive and remain shall be caught up together with them in the clouds, to meet the Lord in the air: and so shall we ever be with the Lord. For which reason comfort one another with these words." *1 Thessalonians 4:15-18*

26. *Rejoice with those who rejoice*

"Rejoice with them that do rejoice" *Romans 12:15*

27. *Weep with those who weep*

"Weep with them that weep." *Romans 12:15 KJV*

28. *Go the second mile*

"Whoever shall compel you to go a mile, go with him two." *Matthew 5:41*

29. *Tell someone their fault one on one*

"Moreover if your brother shall trespass against you, go and tell him his fault between you and him alone: if he shall hear you, you have gained your brother." *Matthew 18:15*

30. *Give a cup of cold water to others*

"Whoever shall give to drink unto one of these little ones a cup of cold water only in the name of a disciple, verily I say unto you, he shall in no wise lose his reward." *Matthew 10:42*

Abraham Lincoln Reading the Bible with His Son

31. *Let your speech be seasoned with grace*

    "Let your speech be always with grace, seasoned with salt" *Colossians 4:6*

32. *Be a peacemaker*

    "Blessed are the peacemakers: for they shall be called the children of God." *Matthew 5:9 KJV*

33. *Do not render evil for evil*

    "Recompense to no man evil for evil." *Romans 12:17 KJV*

34. *Follow good both for yourself and for all*

    "Follow that which is good, both among yourselves, and to all men." *1 Thessalonians 5:15 KJV*

35. *Children of God do righteousness and love*

    "In this the children of God are manifest, and the children of the devil: whoever does not righteousness is not of God, neither he that loves not his brother." *1 John 3:10*

33

36. *Do not show partiality*

"My brethren, have not the faith of our Lord Jesus Christ, the Lord of glory, with respect of persons." *James 2:4 KJV*

37. *Exhort one another*

"But exhort one another daily, while it is called Today; lest any of you be hardened through the deceitfulness of sin." *Hebrews 3:13*

38. *Walk in love*

"Walk in love, as Christ also has loved us, and has given Himself for us" *Ephesians 5:2*

39. *Love the family of God*

"We know that we have passed from death unto life, because we love the brethren." *1 John 3:14 KJV*

40. *Love in act and truth*

"Let us not love in word, neither in tongue; but in deed and in truth." *Hebrews 13:3 KJV*

41. *Have compassion*

"Having compassion one of another" *1 Peter 3:8 KJV*

42. *Share John 3:16 with others*

"For God so loved the world, that He gave His only begotten Son, that whoever believes in Him should not perish, but have everlasting life." *John 3:16*

43. *Be a Good Samaritan (while using wisdom)*

"Which now of these three, think you, was neighbor unto him that fell among the thieves? And he said, He that showed mercy on him. Then said Jesus unto him, Go, and do you likewise." *Luke 10:36-37*

44. *Pray for Christians and pastors to boldly speak of Jesus Christ*

"That I may open my mouth boldly, to make known the mystery of the gospel" *Ephesians 6:19 KJV*

45. *Do not be contentious*

"Not quarrelsome" *1 Timothy 3:3*

46. *Do not be covetous*

"Not covetous" *1 Timothy 3:3 KJV*

47. *Don't threaten*

"Masters, do the same things unto them, forbearing threatening: knowing that your Master also is in heaven; neither is there respect of persons with him. *Ephesians 6:9 KJV*

48. *Pray for your family, church and the USA*

"To comprehend with all saints what is the breadth, and length, and depth, and height; And to know the love of Christ, which passes knowledge" *Ephesians 3:18-19*

49. *Visit orphans and widows*

"Pure religion and undefiled before God and the Father is this, To visit the fatherless and widows in their affliction, and to keep himself unspotted from the world." *James 1:27 KJV*

50. *Do the will of God from your heart*

"Doing the will of God from the heart; With good will doing service, as to the Lord, and not to men" *Ephesians 6:6-7 KJV*

51. *Impart grace to those hearing you speak*

"Let no corrupt communication proceed out of your mouth, but that which is good to the use of edifying, that it may minister grace unto the hearers." *Ephesians 4:29 KJV*

52. *Bear the weaknesses/errors of the weak*

"We then that are strong ought to bear the infirmities of the weak, and not to please ourselves." *Romans 15:1 KJV*

"Be a peacemaker"

Steven Andrew

53. *Give preference to one another*

    "In honor preferring one another"
    Romans 12:10

54. *Have brotherly kindness*

    "Add to your faith... brotherly kindness"
    2 Peter 1:5-7 KJV

55. *Pray for all Christians*

    **"Praying always with all prayer and supplication
    in the Spirit, and watching for this purpose with all
    perseverance and supplication for all saints"**
    Ephesians 6:18 KJV

56. *Be tenderhearted*

    "Tenderhearted" *Ephesians 4:32 KJV*

57. *Beware of wolves in sheep's clothing*

    **"Beware of false prophets, which come to you in
    sheep's clothing, but inwardly they are ravening
    wolves. Ye shall know them by their fruits."**
    Matthew 7:15-16 KJV

58. *Pray for a brother sinning*

    **"If any man see his brother sin a sin which is not
    unto death, he shall ask, and He shall give him life
    for them that sin not unto death. There is a sin
    unto death: I do not say that he shall pray for it."**
    1 John 5:16 KJV

59. *Do not grumble / complain*

    "Grudge not one against another, brethren"
    James 5:9 KJV

60. *Teach the Gospel to faithful men*

"The things that you have heard of me among many witnesses, the same commit you to faithful men, who shall be able to teach others also."
2 Timothy 2:2 KJV

61. *Pray for your family, church and the USA*

"For this cause we also, since the day we heard it, do not cease to pray for you, and to desire that ye might be filled with the knowledge of his will in all wisdom and spiritual understanding"
Colossians 1:9 KJV

62. *Help the weak*

"Support the weak" *1 Thessalonians 5:14 KJV*

63. *Be likeminded toward one another*

"Now the God of patience and consolation grant you to be likeminded one toward another according to Christ Jesus" *Romans 15:5 KJV*

64. *Warn those who are unruly*

"Now we exhort you, brethren, warn them that are unruly" *1 Thessalonians 5:14 KJV*

65. *Be patient*

"Be patient toward all men."
1 Thessalonians 5:14 KJV

66. *Love one another fervently with a pure heart*

"Love one another with a pure heart fervently"
1 Peter 1:22 KJV

67. *Be hospitable*

"Given to hospitality" *1 Timothy 3:2 KJV*

68. *Pray and fast to help others:*

"Jesus rebuked the devil; and he departed out of him: and the child was cured from that very hour... However, this kind goes not out, but by prayer and fasting." *Matthew 17:18-21 KJV*

69. *Do not receive those who speak a different gospel*

"If there come any unto you, and bring not this doctrine, receive him not into your house, neither bid him success: For he that bids success is partaker of his evil deeds." *2 John 10-11*

70. *Minister to one another*

"As every man has received the gift, even so minister the same one to another" *1 Peter 4:10*

71. *Recognize faithful Christian leaders*

"Know them which labor among you, and are over you in the Lord, and admonish you; And to esteem them very highly in love for their work's sake."
1 Thessalonians 5:12-13

72. *Bless those who persecute you*

"Bless them which persecute you: bless, and curse not." *Romans 12:14 KJV*

73. *Lay down your life for the brethren*

"We ought to lay down our lives for the brethren." *1 John 3:16 KJV*

ༀ Family ༄

74. *Decide to serve the LORD*

"As for me and my house, we will serve the LORD." *Joshua 24:15 KJV*

75. *Wife, submit to your husband*

"Wives, submit yourselves unto your own husbands, as unto the Lord." *Ephesians 5:22 KJV*

76. *Wife, respect your husband*

"The wife see that she reverence her husband." *Ephesians 5:33 KJV*

77. *Husband, love your wife*

"Husbands, love your wives, even as Christ also loved the church, and gave himself for it" *Ephesians 5:25 KJV*

78. *Husband, share God's Word with your wife*

"That he might sanctify and cleanse it with the washing of water by the word" *Ephesians 5:26 KJV*

79. *Work out marriage issues - hate divorce*

"For the LORD, the God of Israel, says that He hates putting away: for one covers violence with his garment, says the LORD of hosts" *Malachi 2:16*

80. *Children, obey your parents in the Lord*

"Children, obey your parents in the Lord: for this is right." *Ephesians 6:1 KJV*

81. *Help your parents and grandparents*

"But if any widow have children or nephews, let them learn first to show piety at home, and to repay their parents: for that is good and acceptable before God." *1 Titus 5:4*

82. *Men, rule your house well*

"One that rules well his own house, having his children in subjection with all reverence" *1 Tim. 3:4*

ও More Ways to Love One Another ৵

83. *Love God and keep His commandments*

"By this we know that we love the children of God, when we love God, and keep his commandments."
1 John 5:2 KJV

84. *Walk in the Spirit*

   "Walk in the Spirit" *Galatians 5:16 KJV*

85. *Let your light so shine before men*

   "Let your light so shine before men, that they may see your good works, and glorify your Father which is in heaven." *Matthew 5:16 KJV*

86. *Want others to prosper and be in health*

   "Beloved, I wish above all things that you may prosper and be in health, even as your soul prospers." *3 John 2*

87. *Do not speak evil of one another*

   "Speak not evil one of another, brethren." *James 4:11 KJV*

88. *Do not have hypocrisy*

   "Let love be without hypocrisy." *Romans 12:9*

89. *Have the fruit of the Spirit*

   "But the fruit of the Spirit is love, joy, peace, longsuffering, gentleness, goodness, faith, meekness, temperance: against such there is no law." *Galatians 5:22-23 KJV*

90. *Pray for others*

"That He would grant you, according to the riches of His glory, to be strengthened with might by His Spirit in the inner man" *Ephesians 3:16 KJV*

91. *Speak truth not lies*

"Putting away lying, speak every man truth with his neighbor: for we are members one of another." *Ephesians 4:25*

92. *Consider other people's conscience with your liberty*

"Conscience, I say, not your own, but of the other: for why is my liberty judged of another man's conscience?" *1 Corinthians 10:29*

93. *Speak the truth in love*

"Speaking the truth in love" *Ephesians 4:15 KJV*

94. *End each day in peace*

"Let not the sun go down upon your wrath" *Ephesians 4:26 KJV*

95. *Have compassion*

"Having compassion one of another" *1 Peter 3:8 KJV*

96. *Put away bitterness*

"Let all bitterness, and wrath, and anger, and clamor, and evil speaking, be put away from you, with all malice" *Ephesians 4:31*

97. *Regularly meet with other Christians*

"Not forsaking the assembling of ourselves together" *Hebrews 10:25 KJV*

98. *Be quick to listen*

"Let every man be swift to hear, slow to speak, slow to wrath" *James 1:19 KJV*

99. *Follow peace*

"Follow peace with all men, and holiness, without which no man shall see the Lord... lest any root of bitterness springing up trouble you, and thereby many be defiled" *Hebrews 12:14-15 KJV*

100. *Establish others in their faith*

"To establish you, and to comfort you concerning your faith" *1 Thessalonians 3:2 KJV*

୫୦୶

୫ *Prayer of Salvation* ୶

To become a Christian, pray:

Father,

I confess with my mouth that Jesus Christ is Lord and I believe in my heart that You raised Jesus Christ from the dead. I call upon Jesus to forgive me for my sins. I ask for all the Holy Spirit has to give me so I can walk with You and serve You.

In Jesus' name. Amen.

Pray and read the Bible every day. Jesus loves you.

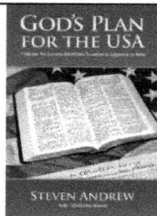

❦ Study Guide ❧

Chapter 1: 100 Ways to Love God
1. What does Mark 12:30 mean?
2. Why have you loved God?
3. How can you love God today?

Chapter 2: 100 Ways to Love One Another
1. Explain what Jesus means in Mark 12:31 and John 13:34.
2. How have you loved as Jesus Christ loved others?
3. What are three new ways you learned to love one another?

Pray: The USA's Covenant with God
Covenant is a holy act. Confess any sins to God before praying.

Father,

You are holy. We thank You that the USA is dedicated to You in covenant to all generations.

LORD, You are the God of the USA and Americans are Your people. We seek You and obey the Holy Bible with all our heart and all our soul. As Jesus is our King, our nation makes Christian disciples and we turn away from everything against Jesus Christ.

We agree with You that the USA is to have marriage as one man and one woman only, have the Bible and Christian prayer in schools, and ban abortion again. We work and pray for covenant Christian leaders to immediately replace those disobeying You.

We thank You for the Cross and by Jesus' blood we receive forgiveness for the USA's sins.

In Jesus' name. Amen.

Psalm 33:12, Mark 12:30, Luke 6:47-49, Isaiah 33:22, Matthew 28:19-20, 2 Timothy 3:5, 2 Chronicles 15, 1 John 1:7. For permission to reprint for non-commercial purposes, include "by Steven Andrew, Pastor of USA Christian Church, www.USA.church".